510
plu

W9-AAX-596

Math Counts

Size

Introduction

In keeping with the major goals of the National Council of Teachers of Mathematics Curriculum and Evaluation Standards, children will become mathematical problem solvers, learn to communicate mathematically, and learn to reason mathematically by using the series Math Counts.

Pattern, Shape, and *Size* may be investigated first—in any sequence.

Sorting, Counting, and *Numbers* may be used next, followed by *Time, Length, Weight,* and *Capacity.*

Ramona G. Choos, Professor of Mathematics, Senior Adviser to the Dean of Continuing Education, Chicago State University; Sponsor for Chicago Elementary Teachers' Mathematics Club

About this Book

Mathematics is a part of a child's world. It is not only interpreting numbers or mastering tricks of addition or multiplication. Mathematics is about *ideas.* These ideas have been developed to explain particular qualities such as size, weight, and height, as well as relationships and comparisons. Yet all too often the important part that an understanding of mathematics will play in a child's development is forgotten or ignored.

Most adults can solve simple mathematical tasks without the need for counters, beads, or fingers. Young children find such abstractions almost impossible to master. They need to see, talk, touch, and experiment.

The photographs and text in these books have been chosen to encourage talk about topics that are essentially mathematical. By talking, the young reader can explore some of the central concepts that support mathematics. It is on an understanding of these concepts that a child's future mastery of mathematics will be built.

Henry Pluckrose

1995 Childrens Press® Edition
© 1994 Watts Books, London, New York, Sydney
All rights reserved.
Printed in the United States of America.
Published simultaneously in Canada.
1 2 3 4 5 6 7 8 9 0 R 04 03 02 01 00 99 98 97 96 95

Math Counts

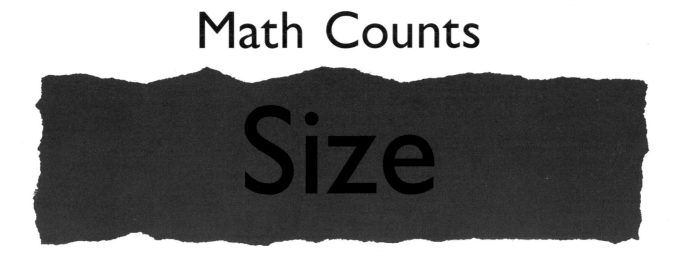

Size

By Henry Pluckrose

Mathematics Consultant: Ramona G. Choos,
Professor of Mathematics

 CHILDRENS PRESS ®
CHICAGO

Do you ever wonder
what words mean?
This is a toy moose.
It is so big
that it is hard to carry.

This baby elephant
is bigger than the toy moose,
but the mother elephant
is the biggest of them all.

This is a toy car.
How do you know that it is too small
to carry people?

This car looks as small as the toy car.
How can you tell that it is bigger?

This is a van.
Do you think it is bigger
or smaller than the car?

This is a double-decker bus.
It carries over 50 people.
It is bigger than the car
and the van.
It is the biggest vehicle.

To know the size of things
we need to have something
to measure them against.
These wheels could be
any size.

It is hard to guess how large
this model might be.
Is it big—or is it small?

We know that this dinosaur is very big indeed.

These fruits are different sizes.
Which is the biggest?
Which is the smallest?

These toy bears are not the same size
Which is bigger? Which is smaller?

Sometimes we need to arrange things in order of size.
These jars are different sizes.

Now they are arranged by size.
The biggest jar is on the left.
The smallest jar is on the right.

We use the words *big* and *small* to describe the size of things.

A rabbit is bigger
than a hamster,

but smaller than a pony.

The pony is a big animal,
but it is smaller than a horse.

The words big and small
help us compare
one thing with another.
A coat can be too big

or too small.
Is the girl too big
for the coat,
or is the coat too small
for the girl?

23

When we buy shoes
we have to make sure
that they are the right size

for the person who is to wear them.

Sometimes we need to make
things appear larger
so that we can see them more easily.
A hornet is a very small creature.
Enlarged, it looks like this.

26

These are raindrops on a leaf.
They also have been enlarged.

Sometimes things seem to be smaller
than they really are.
This airplane looks quite small
when it is high in the sky.

On the ground, it looks much bigger.

How do you know
that this house is big enough
for you to live in,

and that this house has been built for dolls?
What is the biggest thing you can think of?
What is the smallest?

Library of Congress Cataloging-in-Publication Data

Pluckrose, Henry Arthur.
   size / Henry Pluckrose.
     p. cm.
   Originally published: London; New York: F. Watts, 1988.
   (Math counts)
   Includes index.
   Summary: Photographs and text introduce the concepts of size through comparisons.
   ISBN 0-516-05457-0
   1. Size perception — Juvenile literature. 2. Size judgment — Juvenile literature. [1. Size.]
I. Title.
BF299.S5P59 1995
155.4'121411 — dc20   94-38009
                                                           CIP
                                                           AC

Photographic credits: PhotoEdit, © Michael Newman, 4, 31; Chris Fairclough, 5, 6, 8, 9, 10, 11, 14, 15, 16, 17, 21, 22, 23, 24, 25, 27, 29, 30; Unicorn Stock Photos, © V.E. Horne, 7, © Chris Boylan, 18, 20, © Betts Anderson, 19; The Natural History Museum, London 12, 13; ZEFA, 26; Colour Library, © Andrew Rapacz, 28

Editor: Ruth Thomson
Assistant Editor: Annabel Martin
Design: Chloë Cheesman

INDEX